LET'S DRAW STEP BY STEP

Let's Draw
Pets and
Farm Animals

Kasia Dudziuk

WINDMILL
BOOKS

Published in 2017 by **Windmill Books,**
an Imprint of Rosen Publishing
29 East 21st Street, New York, NY 10010

Illustrations: Kasia Dudziuk
Text: JMS Books
Designer: Chris Bell
Editors: Joe Harris and Anna Brett

Cataloging-in-Publication Data
Names: Dudziuk, Kasia.
Title: Let's draw pets and farm animals / Kasia Dudziuk.
Description: New York : Windmill Books, 2017. | Series: Let's draw step by step | Includes index.
Identifiers: ISBN 9781499481792 (pbk.) | ISBN 9781499481808 (library bound) | ISBN 9781508192909 (6 pack)
Subjects: LCSH: Animals in art--Juvenile literature. | Drawing--Technique--Juvenile literature.
Classification: LCC NC783.8.P48 D83 2017 | DDC 743.6--dc23

Manufactured in the United States of America
CPSIA Compliance Information: Batch #BW17PK: For Further Information contact Rosen Publishing, New York, New York at 1-800-237-9932

Contents

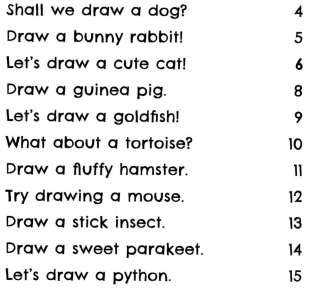

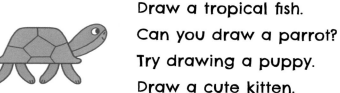

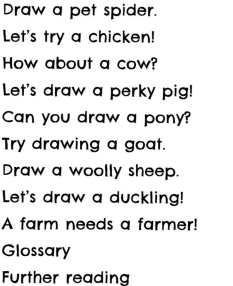

Shall we draw a dog?

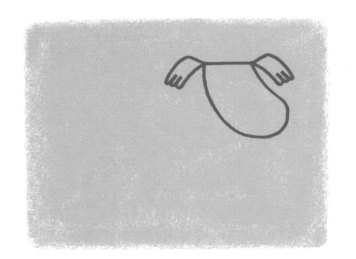

1 Start with his head and floppy ears.

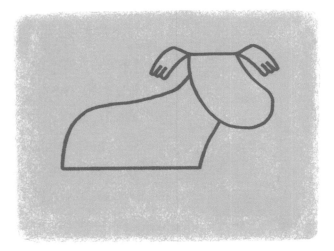

2 Now draw his body.

3 Add his tail and legs.

4 Add his face and color his furry coat.

Draw a bunny rabbit!

1 Draw his head and long ears.

2 Now give him a body.

3 Add shapes for his legs.

4 He has a cute face and a fluffy white tail!

Let's draw a cute cat!

1 First draw her head and ears.

2 Now draw her body.

3 She needs legs and a long curly tail.

4 Add her face, color her coat and she's done!

Your cat could be orange, black, white or gray.

Can you draw a cat sitting down?

1 Start with her head again.

2 This time her body is angled.

3 Add her front legs and tail.

4 There, she's finished!

You can draw lots of different cats!

Draw a guinea pig.

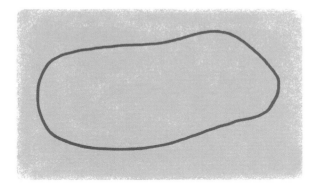

1 Draw this shape for his head and body.

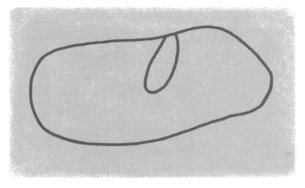

2 Now draw his cute floppy ear.

3 He has little legs and feet.

4 Draw his face and whiskers, and color his soft fur.

Let's draw a goldfish!

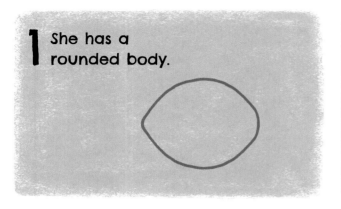
1 She has a rounded body.

2 Add some fins to help her swim.

3 Draw her tail and a side fin.

4 A goldfish should be gold!

Why not draw a glass bowl for your goldfish?

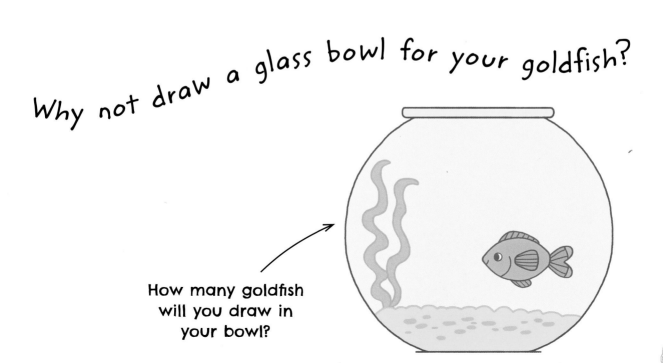

How many goldfish will you draw in your bowl?

What about a tortoise?

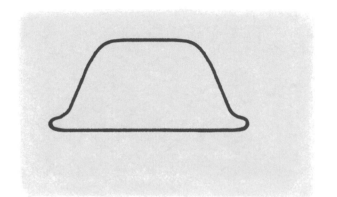

1 Let's start by drawing his shell.

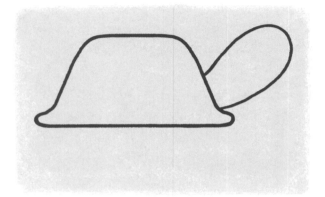

2 He has a long neck.

3 Now draw his four stumpy legs.

4 Color him any shade you like!

Why not draw your tortoise munching on some lettuce?

Draw a fluffy hamster.

1 Start with his head and little ears.

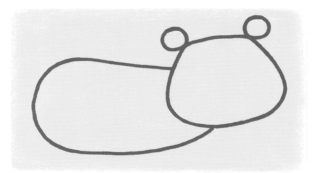

2 Add his rounded body.

3 He has little legs and a stumpy tail.

4 Draw his face and color in his fluffy coat!

Can you draw a wheel for your hamster to play in?

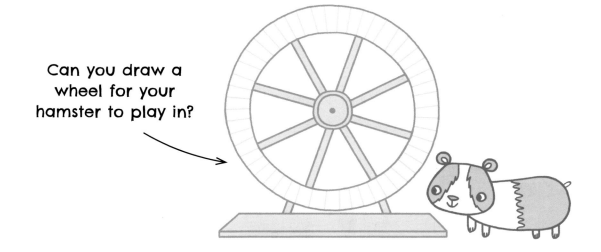

Try drawing a mouse.

1 He has two round ears and a pointed head.

2 Now add his body.

3 Draw his legs so that he is running. Don't forget his long tail!

4 Draw his face, feet and whiskers. Color him gray.

Draw a stick insect.

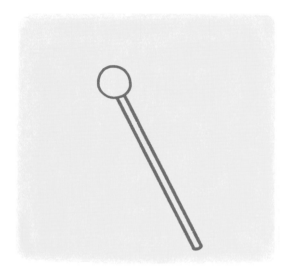

1 Start by drawing his round head and long body. It looks just like a stick!

2 Now add three thin legs on the left side of his body...

3 ...and three thin legs on the right side!

4 Give him some antennae and a nice smiley face. Color him green.

Draw a sweet parakeet.

1 Here is his feathery head.

2 Now he has a feathery wing.

3 Add his legs and a long tail!

4 Draw his face and feet. Isn't he a handsome bird?

Let's draw a python.

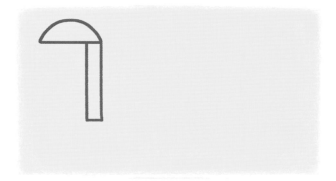

1 Start with a semicircle for his head, and a long neck.

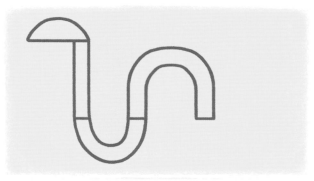

2 Add two U-shapes to make coils for his body...

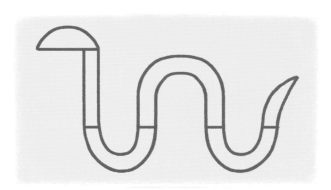

3 ...and another coil, before finishing with his tail.

4 Give him an eye and a forked tongue. Add a zigzag pattern to his body and color him shades of green.

Can you draw a coiled python?

Draw a tropical fish.

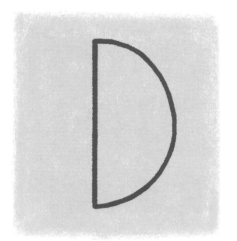

1 Start with his body shape.

2 Add his nose and tail.

3 He needs fins to help him swim.

4 Give him some bright stripes!

Can you draw a whole shoal of pretty fish?

Can you draw a parrot?

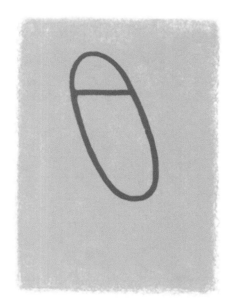

1 Here are her body and head.

2 Now she has a beak and feet.

3 She needs wings and feathers!

4 Add her tail, an eye and choose some pretty colors.

Try drawing a puppy.

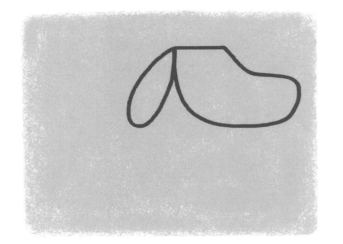

1 Start with his head and one floppy ear.

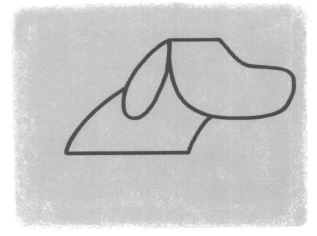

2 Now draw his body.

3 He needs four legs.

4 Draw his face and tail and color him in.

Draw a cute kitten.

1 Draw her round head and little pointed ears.

2 Add this curly shape for her back leg.

3 She needs front legs and a big fluffy tail!

4 Draw her face and color her in. This kitten has gray fur.

Draw a pet spider.

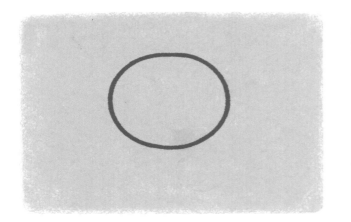

1 First draw a round shape for her body.

2 Add four wriggly legs on her left side...

3 ...and another four legs on her right side.

4 Draw her face and color her black.

Let's try a chicken!

1 This is her body and head.

2 Add her beak and feathers.

3 Don't forget her legs and wing.

4 Add her feet and color her in. She has a very beady eye!

She needs a cozy henhouse!

How about a cow?

1 She has a large head and little ears.

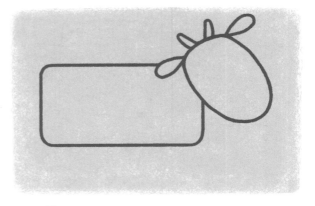

2 Add her horns. Her body is like a rectangle.

3 She needs legs and a tail – almost finished!

4 Draw her face and color her with pretty patches of light brown.

You can make your cow black and white if you prefer!

Let's draw a perky pig!

1 He has a nice round head and snout.

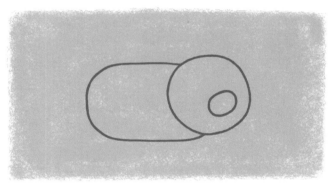

2 Now draw his body.

3 He needs legs and ears.

4 Don't forget his face and his curly tail!

Can you draw a pony?

1 First draw his body.

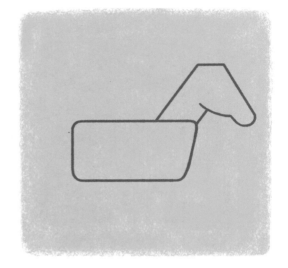

2 Then add his head.

3 He needs ears and long legs.

4 He has a lovely long tail and a mane!

Can you draw different types of ponies?

Color this pony brown.

A pony with patches is called a "piebald."

A unicorn has a long shiny horn.

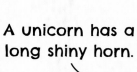

Pegasus is a flying horse. He needs some wings.

Try drawing a goat.

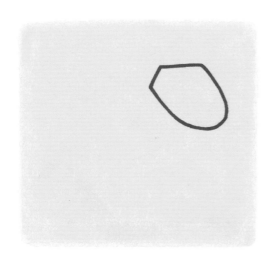

1 Here is his head.

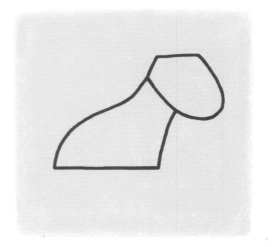

2 Now draw his body.

3 Add his little ears and legs.

4 Draw his face, and two curly horns. Then color him in.

Draw a woolly sheep.

1 Let's start with his head.

2 Add his body and ears.

3 He needs legs and a little tail!

4 Draw his face and give him a woolly coat.

Let's draw a duckling!

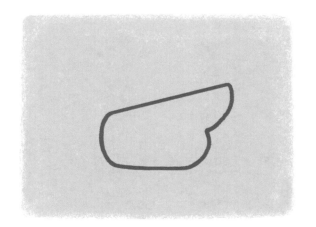

1 Let's start with his body.

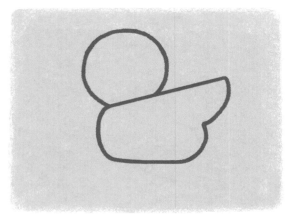

2 Add a round head on top.

3 He needs a beak and two webbed feet.

4 Give him an eye and a wing and color him in.

To show your duck swimming, draw the water and splashes like this.

A farm needs a farmer!

1 First draw his head.

2 Now add his body, arms and legs.

3 He needs some clothes!

4 Give him a face and some nice red boots!

Glossary

antennae Two long, thin body parts on the head of insects and other animals, used to feel and smell.

fin A flat part of the body of a fish used for balance and swimming.

goldfish A small yellow or orange fish that lives in freshwater.

guinea pig A small animal with short legs, no tail and soft fur.

hamster A small animal with a round body, short tail and pouches in its cheeks.

parakeet A small parrot with very bright feathers and a pointed tail.

Pegasus A horse with wings that is not real but comes from Greek stories.

python A snake that lives in Africa and likes to wrap itself around its food.

stick insect An insect that looks like a twig.

tortoise A reptile that lives on the land.

tropical fish Fish with bright colors that often live in a fish tank.

unicorn A horse from storybooks that has a long horn on its forehead.

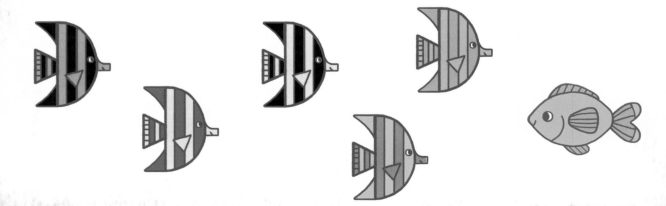

Further reading

How to Draw Animals by Leone Pratt (Usborne Publishing Ltd, 2014)

It's Fun to Draw Pets by Mark Bergin (Sky Pony Press, 2014)

Junior How to Draw Baby Animals by Kate Thompson (Top That Publishing, 2011)

Learn to Draw Farm Animals by Jickie Torres and Robbin Cuddy (Walter Foster, 2011)

Usborne Step-by-Step Drawing Animals by Fiona Watt (Usborne Publishing Ltd, 2015)

Websites

For web resources related to the subject of this book, go to:
www.windmillbooks.com/weblinks and select this book's title.

Index